P

THE CONVERT'S HEART
IS GOOD TO EAT

"Melody S. Gee's gorgeous poems offer both divine wounds and delicious consolations. At the intersections of the familial and the sacred, *The Convert's Heart is Good to Eat* reminds us that what is created is also consumed. Beautiful, sensory, and aching, this collection reminds us that not all hungers are mortal ones."

— Traci Brimhall, author of *our lady of the ruins*

"What happens when the call of spirit utterly changes a life? 'To be consoled begins with grief,' Melody S. Gee writes, and I think about that prefix, con: how it means 'with' in Latin; how Gee's book is a chronicle of being with: with God, and with parents, children, and the old self, in the light of new faith. I thought too of the word concord— to 'heart' with another. How do I walk in concord? This is the primary question of Gee's moving book.

— Dana Levin, author of *Now Do You Know Where You Are*

"Melody S. Gee's *The Convert's Heart Is Good to Eat* is a book of captivating intensity and precision. This compact collection reveals a talent and range that are rare in recent books of poems by American poets. Deeply evocative, Gee's lyric meditations on motherhood, being a daughter, and on how one shapes a voice for an adult convert are as necessary as food and water for the living soul."

— Eugene Gloria, author of *Sightseer in this Killing City*

"These are gorgeous poems of hunger and grace. Melody S. Gee explores the convert's relationship with faith and who we become through conversion. She crafts grief and loss into a new kind of knowing, how 'a spill will always take a shape, a floating/map of damage.' *The Convert's Heart is Good to Eat* is a feast, a welcome arrival, a stellar book to savor and devour."

— Lee Herrick, author of *Scar and Flower*

"Through the poetry of desire and faith, of motherhood and childhood, Melody S. Gee's *The Convert's Heart Is Good to Eat* offers an unflinching exploration of how the flesh and the spirit suffer wounds and yearn to be healed. These poems create and undo themselves in the most surprising and loveliest of ways. This book will make you believe."

— W. Todd Kaneko, author of *This Is How the Bone Sings*

THE CONVERT'S HEART IS GOOD TO EAT

MELODY S. GEE

INDEPENDENTLY PUBLISHED BY
DRIFTWOOD PRESS

Independently published by Driftwood Press
in the United States of America.

Managing Poetry Editor: Jerrod Schwarz
Poetry Editors: Andrew Hemmert & Kimberly Povloski
Guest Judge: Traci Brimhall
Cover Image: Max Emanuel Ainmiller
Cover Design: Sally Franckowiak,
Jerrod Schwarz, & James McNulty
Innards Design: Jerrod Schwarz
Copyeditor: Jerrod Schwarz & James McNulty
Fonts: Merriweather, Maecenas, & Modesto Text

First published on June 28th, 2022
ISBN-13: 978-1-949065-17-6

Please visit our website at www.driftwoodpress.net
or email us at editor@driftwoodpress.net

CONTENTS

For Paul, Bea, and Josie

THE CONVERT LEARNS TO PLAY HIDE AND SEEK

The convert hid within her grandfather's
restaurant while her cousin hunted,
while their mothers fried in oil and sweet

and sour. When the convert's parents
laid eyes on her they said, *daughter, daughter.*
They never played this game with her

because from *daughter* there is no hiding.
When the Lord walked in the garden calling
the pair from the trees, a game began.

Now the convert strains to find Him, fingering
her ripped places, stalking Him out of His
relentless camouflage.

The theologian says there is no faith
without separation. A ship will sink
under its own lighthouse.

Now the convert's daughter is hiding from her.
The girl knows being found is the part
you wait for but is not the best part.

Tucked behind the restaurant's lard buckets,
the convert heard the boy flushing
the usual traps and dark passages.

She entered a country where she thought
she could live. The writer says *waiting* is
etymologically related to *vigor*, to *vigilance*.

The convert seeks with bellows and stomps.
Her daughter's laughs reveal her place
every time. Who can keep from saying *here I am*?

LITURGY

Even celery slices and chicken cubes
for the sake of even cooking time.
The bias cut looks elegant and sautés

faster. The quarter steer is readied
for carryout. Fillet until thumb sized.
A guest must cut nothing for herself.

Measure oil in ladles, salt in palms.
A slide of sugar tames the bitter.
Only balance will sate. If you crave
the meal was lopsided.

The eye and hand flavor precisely,
but into the cartons dishes must
overflow. Fill rice over the lip.
A strained seal says, *see how much*

was poured out for you?
Three chunks of pineapple
and a scattering of sesame seeds

is all the gloss a sweet and sour
pork carton will need.
The meat is fried twice after closing
in lard rendered from silk

to blistering. Near dawn,
my mother peels back thin socks
altered to arm bands, weeding
her burns of polyester threads.

Your dish is scooped from seven
different buckets of evenly diced
and coded parts. You watch

the muscle memory of women
with ossified tongues and unbound feet.
Their noontime chant: *fill, fill, fill*.

The door opens and a bell calls out
hunger at vespers, at holy hour.
Decades of automation lift the hands
that offer you and receive you.

THE CONVERT DESIRES HER WAY INTO A FIRST PRAYER

Her mother's first lesson
was chew your wants and spit

the pulp, grow skinny feeding
everyone else your flesh.

A heart's cargo is sometimes oil,
sometimes crude. A spill can undo

the waterproof of any surface.
And still the diving birds must feed,

must point their beaks past the slick
that seals the cornea to eternal blur.

Does the Lord ask her what she wants
when he already knows its name?

Does he play these games to make her
ignorant tongue collapse?

A spill will always take a shape, a floating
map of damage. In the cleanup,

particles separate from the main
and cast out into fish

bellies and clam adductors.
What do you want me to do for you,

He asks. Her cargo is not
contaminate. Her answers clear water.

Let me oil. Let me wash.
Let me want with a full throat

even of hopeless warbling.
Let You do nothing about any of it.

Let each desire form in this mouth
whose teeth You have taken from me.

AND SO MORE

Begin with before you
are made. Fat gold
watch tinkered
together, overwound.

A blossom becomes when
the tree says, when air says.
The nectar before the bee
before the eager comb—

whose are all
these materials?

Your early cells would
be anything. Some directive
says *heart* and not *nail*,
so the cells divide, each

split extinguishes *lip*, *vessel*,
iris, to build the heart's walls.
You are separation, neither
pieced nor built.

When the light came away
from darkness, the darkness
did not ease. Neither the sea
when land slouched up.

And so on. And so more.

Tell me, on what day
was your hunger cleaved
from thirst?
On what day did wailing
form in your liquid lungs?

CONDITIONS

The red bean can't tear open to
root until it eats all the growth
inhibitors swaddling the hibernating seed,
until the right climate says *yield*.

In school we line beans into damp bags
to sprout. We gaze and prod them: break
and burrow without light. And

they do. We watch root and stem, equally
furious, extending. In little baggies among second
grade clutter, the sprouts go
forth not knowing up from down.

By winter, I already know how to eat
my armor. Neither do I want to enter
the world under these conditions.

What can come from a chewed hull,
from the body set free by its own
careful devouring?

Weeks later we find the bags, slick
and rot-clouded. Not green,
not plant, these bloodless filaments

spiraling nowhere, pale as fingernails.
Every cell's engine had waited for the light
we sealed out. Every multiplication

a miracle: instructions followed nevertheless.

THE CONVERT RECEIVES THE SIGN OF THE CROSS
ON HER FEET

The immigrants' daughter doesn't know Easter
      or egg hunts.
            Someone cuts a starting line

ribbon to unleash the gatherers and she is washed
      into the herd. She knows
she is supposed to seek.

      No one has told her these eggs will not be
          the raw, white ones

      her dutiful mother tucked by the longbeans.
She doesn't know to spot silver wrappings
      or shiny plastics.

She is turned around, lapping a brick path with
      her basket, some centerpiece
with dented floral foam still packed in the bottom.

      She doesn't notice others yanking at grasses
or parting bushes like curtains.
         Her mother has taught her never to take.

      To initiate her into mystery, the convert receives
         the sign of the cross

on her eyes, her ears, her lips, her shoulders,
      her hands, her heart. She replies
I am to every question.

      Then her husband kneels
and thumbs a cross on each foot.
         She cannot remember the priest's words

          for why but hears him call her catechumen.
        Her feet, barely sandaled, receive their signs
    on skin and bones.

The hunt stretches on and she knows much lies
        beyond her, scattered and hidden, but also
nowhere. In the exit line, a smiling

        host puts three bright eggs in her empty basket
and pats her shoulder.

                Aisles pulse at communion.
                        The convert watches them open their hands
        and mouths, how they vanish the wine

together. She wonders if
        the sip stains the wafer before it melts,
                if that steep is enough

        to change the body's contours
as it eases down to fill the fast.

LOVE OUTNUMBERS US

My girl presents sliced flesh for me to mend.
Wound tending surges the site with pain. But

pain exposed will blend with tender fingers
sealing the bandage over salve, over

her body's steady repair. Tended pain
leaps, but then alights, tethered suddenly

to relief. She sighs when I say *ouch* like
I too am winced open. Her flesh unfolds

and the light enters. This she remembers.
How else does she know, with barely any

words herself, to tend her new sister, clucking
and crooning *oh no no* at each bright yelp.

The sister sleeping beside her, who knows
inside their slack dark they are two. I am

an only child, aflame with envy.
To give what I missed is consolation.

To be consoled begins with grief. What was
never mine is still somehow mine to give,

can somehow be divided among us.
Love outnumbers us with its roughhewn stones

quarried in parcels big as we can bear
or some other size.

THE CONVERT WANTS WOUNDS, NOT SCARS

The wound on her lip goes white
before returning red.

The virus erupts the lines between chin
and lip, between lip and philtrum.

A sore across two continents
of skin, a bridge of lava.

She will feel healed when the flesh
color returns. The variation

is the aberration. Blood courses
to deliver a clot. Vessels

bouquet under the scalp or in
the womb, in places where we

heal fastest. Over the wound
cells scramble a lean-to

scab, a mortar of new skin.
The body wants to draw

its seams together.
But Jesus hangs before

the convert eternally
wounded, eternally weeping

from his gashes.
How to open hers without nails

or thorns? How to measure
heartbeats without seeing

blood heave out its rhythms?
A gush slows under

pressure even as the pulse
goes on. Our lesions take air, our

infections seek sunlight. How to
resist our unwilled mechanisms

to staunch? We push through the same
tear in the world and leave it sore.

When we come, we come open.

Pick a wound slow to bleed
and slower to seal. We cream

the scar to fade our atlas of living—
what itched its way to a silver road,

what shadow constellation of pox.
The convert counts Jesus' wounds.

If you count both hands and both feet,
all lashes and piercings

and the forsaken cry, the number
is higher and lower than anyone's.

LEARN TO WALK

Fawn, an open

meadow is spread
with harm.

Every clearing stir

twitches the ear,
the follicles cup

every rustle. Your abrupt

posture prepared
to spring. A life alert.

How fast blood

must pump to stay
this ready. Your body

enters the clearing

tracked and scoped.
And yet the clover.

The goldenrod. The flush

of acorns says surrender
your alarm.

Take your cover

with you. Your spots
have not yet darkened

into hide.

THE CONVERT RECEIVES THE SACRAMENTS
WITH FLOWING WATER

What fills the font is not
drawn from river

whose deltas are gnarled
silt knuckles clenched

against salt laps.
Farther back

from deltas, humans
wash and slake and piss

and baptize. Water
distressed and returned

gritted and grimed.
For her sacrament, indoors

and unwild, water must
flow by priest's application.

Locust and honey
are not for luncheon.

The convert's first shard
of full moon altar

bread refuses dissolution.
The first dark sip

fumes her throat and ignites
below. Chrism gleams

her pores to reflecting pools.
A glint of light always thinks

it is God, even slick parking
lot runoff, even gutter stream

and blessed gems of balsam and olive
oil cry miracle. Still water knows

gravity gathers, knows how floodplain
and watershed will always

receive. In a river afire
with fish or a font that catches

what hands pour, the world
ripples and then it stills, all
flesh and foul and hunger.

MOTHER TONGUE

1.
A chrysalis vibrates in you
but will not erupt wings.

Your teacher thinks
the butterfly is coming

any day now. I tell you
the child's name.

Your chrysalis says impossible.
You learn to call her something

else. Your mouth
an utter betrayal.

2.
A surgery will untie
the infant's tongue so she
can milk.
A mutilation for
unfettered quenching.

3.
A caterpillar's DNA does not
exit the cocoon. Wings form
from the soup of the old body.

The shell carries a name.
But what do we call
the cauldron inside?

4.
In every throat the passage for air
closes when food nears.
We cannot consume and

respire, we cannot take in
all at once.

5.
Wings heave in brute escape
from the self-spun womb.
The new creature is not
a version. A few
nectared months,
a flight of milkweed,
a life.

6.
Not everything that trembles
your tongue or your throat
is a voice.

QUESTIONS FOR AN IMMIGRANT'S CHILD

What does this mean
How do you say this   But what
does it mean
How can you go
What do you owe
for this life

How do you write this
How do you have
so much
How has it not made you
less selfish   How do you

talk to us like that   Do I
say it this way   How does
a map work   How do I tell
time
How come you don't taste
as you cook   How do you know
anything is good

How come you go
Do you like
to make me worry   Why
not wait   How do you say
what you think all
the time   All these words how
come you don't
call

What number is this   How many
in a pound   Why are these
so expensive
Why do you have
to talk so fast
You hear me   You listening
What else could I do

THE CONVERT'S HEART IS GOOD TO EAT

The girl and her mother are seekers
of water. They catch drips from a broken
aloe sword. A wide cactus mitt oozes

clear medicine. Tendril roots purify
along blind channels hurtling toward
blossom, toward the bright ovary
picked for its blush.

What happens inside a body happens
in darkness. Nothing to guide the cells'
churning and dying, or tug blood on

its course. Nothing but scribbled echoes
to expose an unborn face within the caul.

The convert's heart is a fruit cased in rind.
Is it the kind with a ragged stone in its throat?
Or with seeds woven in each wedge of flesh?

Is it the kind webbed with bitter pith and oil?
The convert's heart hangs low for gathering
and open to the animal bargain of sugar.

The daughter sees the heart, ever on display
and swollen with light. Ever thirst and
appetite ripened to sweetest grief.

WHETHER AND

> "It's nothing to me
> Who gathers in us."
> —Harvey Shapiro, "Notes at 46"

There you are, nothing
to me. Who gathers you

in handfuls, who sews
you down my back?

You are something
now, out of the shape of just

a cell, all from
impulse, from heat.

You grow and divide grow
and divide.

The ground winters
you, splits your seed,

crawls its minerals up into
your passages. Empty as

I came, I grow your skeleton.
I am hungry. I am feeding.

In winter, sap falls still
but roots never stop suckling.

The glassy loam, the decay in
frigid stillness still crumbles

the living. A press of white birds
hush over us. We feel the temperature

as a number. The whether and where
of you is what to me?

You lie unlived inside
unready to bulb.

Whether and where you go
or come, whether yes,

whether us, whether what lies
is still singing.

SOMETHING OUTSIDE MYSELF

a conversation with Melody S. Gee and Jerrod Schwarz

Let me start off by saying how much of a joy it's been to read and publish this chapbook, Melody! I want to begin our discussion by looking at one of the chapbook's major concerns: the intersection of faith and identity. Specifically, I'm struck by how these poems investigate stark symbols of American Christianity (easter eggs, stigmata, sacraments) through the lens of childhood. What aspects of this belief system felt crucial to include in your chapbook? Inversely, were there any elements of this faith that you chose to exclude?

Thanks, Jerrod! This is thrilling for me.

I'm looking at Catholicism through the lens of an adult convert. I received my first sacraments at age thirty five, after three years of seeking and discerning within the church. My conversion surprised me as much as anyone, and I've been trying to understand it since it began in early 2013.

I've known callings before—to writing, to mother-hood—but faith pulled me in quickly, unexpectedly, and hard. The demands were part of the attraction. At times, I felt positively pursued—by the Gospel, the numinous, the awe, the obligations to love everyone as you love yourself. Something in me just keeps saying yes.

These poems are my trying to ask and answer the questions of what I am doing and who I am becoming in conversion. I look to my childhood for clues, but as the daughter of Chinese immigrants, my family was non-re-ligious. However, there was a spirituality in our home. We lived among the dead—ancestors whose presence in and effect on our lives was real. Nearly everything we ate, wore, did, or said could influence our fortune, which hinged on our ancestors' appeasement or wrath. In some ways, I was primed for a life of faith. The poem, "The Convert Receives the Sign of the Cross on Her Feet" is trying to comb the past for traces of faith or gaps that faith is trying to fill. I think I'm searching for a cohesive narrative that includes and perhaps explains this unexpected turn. I'm trying to see if the girl is the same since the convert was born, to see if the story is big enough to contain them both.

There are so many ways that faith feels like a rejection

of my past—this sense of betrayal was the hardest thing for me to reconcile, and the reason receiving my sacraments took so long. I was raised to avoid and fear strangers; my faith teaches me to encounter them. I was raised to save and build wealth; my faith asks me to give it away. I was raised to deny my desires; my faith says that desires are God's gift and voice. I was raised with filial piety as my ultimate concern; my faith pushes me out beyond. So, yes, the book is concerned with faith and identity because I'm living the tension of a change that is part of my life and my entire life. What does conversion mean for my past? What does it do to the "before?" Is there room for all the past and the present? Does a new ultimate concern mean a rejection of another? In truth, my conversion haunts me. I wrestle with what it's asking of me. Sometimes I feel like I'm gathering my past to me, reassuring it that it will not be abandoned.

I love your phrasing here, that spiritual conversions and affirmations of faith can "haunt" us. These are obviously massive metaphysical inquiries, but I wondered if you would be able to share how your writing has evolved post-conversion. Perhaps more specifically, how have the daily writing and spiritual practices coalesced?

There are parallels to my writing and spiritual lives, especially in my daily practices. I don't write every day. For me, it's not a reality with working and having kids. But I do work on my writing every day. Sometimes it's committing time to read, listen to a rich podcast, journal, meet with a friend—doing things that feed me with language and connection. Much the same is true for my faith life. It's rare that I get a length of time to sit contemplatively, but I get the daily gospel in my email, go for a walk, work in ministries at my parish—things that push me toward prayer and connection.

While I long for stretches of uninterrupted time, and I do give that to myself in the form of retreats or sabbaticals, I try to not separate my life into "family"; "work"; "spiritual"; or "writing" anymore, so time doesn't feel scarce or competitive. Fifteen minutes of revision between client calls isn't a failure or a cheat. Meeting a friend for lunch on a weekday isn't stealing from work time. The absolute hardest part of my writing and spiritual discipline is to stop asking, *What do I have?* and ask instead, *What am*

I in the presence of? I succeed and fail, get resentful, and feel defeated all the time. What sustains me is my community—my small circle of incredible writers and my parish community. When I get too much in my head trying to control or bargain or excel my way into dominating time, it's Mass or a writing meetup that pull me back. Their gifts are the same—I am made part of something larger and outside myself.

These poems are largely delivered through a unified speaker, but they still span multiple generations, with motherhood being a key focus. What are the challenges and joys inherent in writing about these profound relationships?

I guess I'm haunted as much by motherhood as conversion. As an adoptee, I know the longings, breaks, limitations, and grief of motherhood through the eyes of a daughter. As a mom of two biological daughters, I understand these even more keenly now. Beginning with pregnancy, I have known motherhood as paradox: intimacy and separation; growing and dying; shelter and exposure; betrayal of daughterhood. I write about motherhood because it is a constant negotiation of identity, desire, love, sacrifice, envy, fear, and mystery.

The parent–child relationship was easily defined when I was a child. My role was obedience and service, to take care of my parents. This duty is heightened for children of immigrants who have to help their parents navigate the English–speaking world. To be an independent, separate person, I can't occupy that role the way they want me to anymore, and it's both necessary and a betrayal. When I became a mom, I knew my daughter and I needed to exist separately and still be intimately connected. I write about motherhood to answer the questions, *Who am I to you? Who are you to me?* These are the same questions I ask God.

This is a powerful distinction that rings true in these poems, the idea that maturity and growth can be at the same time personally essential and negatively felt by others. To that point, have you noticed any shifts in writing as the role of daughter and mother starts to switch?

Becoming a mom transformed how I understood my own childhood and gave me access to write about it in new ways. One example is when my oldest daughter turned nine months old, I was hit by a profound grief at seeing how much she understood and could communicate by that age, how much her world and her identity had been built, because I was adopted at nine months old. I thought about what must be lost at that age, even in the best adoption circumstances.

My daughters bring me back to myself like this all the time. When they ask about their birth stories and coo over their own baby pictures, expressing love for the person they once were, I see them integrating the self that existed before they knew themselves. In telling them their birth stories a thousand times, I realized how deep the same need was in me, only I didn't ask questions about my origin. My family's single narrative was the typical and most acceptable one about adoption—being chosen and lucky. While those are part of the story, there's also grief, loss, and a constant shadow of *what-if*. When I'm taken back to that part of my story, I feel more integrated myself, and newly able to write about what had previously felt inaccessible to me.

There is a harrowing balance of tenderness and violence in these poems. One haunting section calmly states "Fawn, an open / meadow is spread / with harm." As an editor, I am always fascinated by a poet's process for rendering dense and complex topics in their writing. How conscious or subconscious were these themes when you set out writing these poems?

The theme of danger is a conscious one for me. Safety and exposure are things my immigrant family worried about. Our take-out restaurant was our livelihood, and it felt easily and continually threatened. People vandalized the restaurant, broke in, left without paying, threatened to call the health department or tell people we served cat meat just because they didn't like the food, or shamed us for not speaking English well. Institutions were hostile too—the health department, the police, the IRS. Most days, it felt like us against the world. I am used to armor and isolation as responses to danger and uncertainty.

As a mom, I have to confront risk beyond myself, and I have to let go of armor and isolation. My greatest love and my worst fear are walking around today in 8- and 11-year-old bodies. "Learn to Walk" is the most explicit about how mothers navigate risk and the strain of my ambivalence about protecting them. Every moment can feel like this: the fawn eager for the meadow that is brimming with sustenance and danger. The choice is between hiding, which means safety and starvation, or exposure, which means nourishment, learning to walk, and being hunted. How do we make our calculations? How do we discern natural desire from temptation?

One of the things that attracts me to Catholicism is the emphasis on the human body and all the risks that entails. Mary experiences pregnancy and childbirth. Jesus is born amid animals and lives the whole of human experience, including hunger, astonishment, pity, pain, grief, fear, abandonment, death. Our liturgy involves eating, drinking, singing, anointing the body with oil. The world is sacramental. Kathleen Norris writes, "The Incarnation remains a scandal to anyone who wants religion to be a purely spiritual matter...It remains a scandal to Christians who fear and despise the human body." My struggle with all of this vulnerability, with tolerating mystery, with not being in control, is the place I write from.

It's interesting to hear how many parallels exist between a writing life and a spiritual one, especially your thoughts on mystery and vulnerability. I admit to not knowing too many Catholic theologians or thinkers, but I've always been struck by the Merton Prayer and how he opens with "I have no idea where I am going." In terms of what's next for you, are there any vulnerabilities or mysteries that you want to dive into next?

That is one of my favorite prayers! While it is starkly honest about doubt, it is one of the most grounded prayers I know. Merton calls out to "My Lord God" even while he wrestles with not knowing what he is doing. There is such deep trust alongside that vulnerability and uncertainty.

Part of my next project, a book of essays on my conversion, is writing about parent-child attachment, adoption, and faith. I've had a hard time with images of God as parent—that is not a grammar I find natural. I'm also writing about different forms of grief—from adoption, immigration, disruptions in attachment, alienation. Aside from vulnerable topics, I find writing in prose and putting together a longer project pretty daunting. Writing a book proposal scares the daylights out of me.

I'm in my forties now, and my kids are tweens and

very independent. My freelance work is steady, and I'm in control of my projects and my time. I feel like all the rush of life has quieted down. I'm done advancing my career, saving for a house, or chasing after little kids. So much of what I worked to build has been built and can be simply enjoyed. The quiet is terrifying, but it's inviting and beautiful too. I don't miss the hustling, but its absence makes me nervous, like I don't know how to gauge the value of what I'm doing without external pressure. One of the next vulnerabilities I'm turning toward is the midlife transformation of urgency into the work of waiting (this is also terrifying).

When I set out to write an interview, one of my favorite ways to investigate a poet's work is to look at word frequency. Now, word frequency does not always directly correlate to author intention, but I think it can reveal interesting insights. In your chapbook, *I* appears sixteen times, but *you* shows up nearly forty times. While these poems certainly feel confessional, there is a powerful exteriority being revealed as well. One of my favorite stanzas reads "There you are, nothing / to me. Who gathers you". How do you see the speaker functioning in these poems? How did the speaker of these poems evolve from their first drafts?

There are several different *you* figures in the poems: God, the unborn, the fawn, the immigrant parent, the immigrant's child, the convert. I hope the address and dialogue contribute to the poems' confessional feel and intimacy. At the same time, the figure of the convert offers a way to explore my own faith journey with some distance, to try and interrogate my experiences from outside myself. I didn't think all these poems would work together until I read Charles Yu's novel *Interior Chinatown*, which achieves piercing interiority through the distance of a screenplay and imagined performance.

I think the exteriority is a recent development in my writing. Usually, I write by tunneling into myself, trying to find language for an intensity of feeling. Then I shape the poem for a reader after there are some guts on the page. I draw out the feeling with place, sensory detail, question, action, story, and hopefully fresh language. But the story of the convert is something I myself find curious—strange, even. The convert poems got composed very differently. I looked at my catechumen ceremony or my baptism to figure them out, sometimes wondering if they really happened, if they happened to me. I needed to figure out what conversion reshapes, redefines, and changes. In doing so, these poems end up telling her story. I'm not trying to pretend it isn't my story, but the distance felt right and needed to hold all of the curiosity, awe, fear, and guilt that conversion has meant for me.

I love this, the idea that a pathway to the intimately confessional includes second-guessing and even dissociation; I am always most excited by poetry that truly grapple with its concerns, and your poems do not shy away from the very questions they ask. To that end, are there any themes or concerns in this chapbook that you will want to return to? Inversely, are there any aspects that you want to set aside?

I'm not setting aside any topics specifically. I'm grateful for whatever moves me to write. I'm not yet done writing about conversion. I hope to finish a memoir project about it next year. I think I'll always write about immigration, adoption, motherhood, and nature. If my family is reading this, they are laughing because they know I don't actually like to be in nature—I much prefer the indoors and only maybe will venture onto a screened-in porch. But it's our relationship to nature and the unseen mechanisms of nature that work in and on us that I'll always write about.

NOTES

pg 7 – Paul Tillich's *The Dynamics of Faith* and Kathleen Norris' *Acedia and Me*

pg 5 – The first stanza takes a line from Sylvia Plath's "Morning Song"

ACKNOWLEDGEMENTS

Grateful acknowledgement to the journals and magazines where the following poems first appeared:

"The Convert Wants Wounds, Not Scars" *Academy of American Poets* Poem-a-Day, 2019
"And So More" *Lantern Review*, 2019
"Learn to Walk" *The Rappahannock Review*, 2019
"The Convert's Heart is Good to Eat" *Ruminate*, 2018
"Liturgy" *Slippery Elm*, 2017
"The Convert Learns to Play Hide and Seek" and "The Convert Desires Her Way into a First Prayer" *Figure One*, 2017

————————————————————

Thank you to Kundiman for my writing home. Thank you to my parents, my parish family, and my St. Louis writing family. Thank you to my daughters, Beatrice and Josephine, for being my light and music. Thank you to Paul for being the prayer I say and the answer I receive.

C. Smyth Photography

Melody S. Gee is the author of *The Dead in Daylight* (Cooper Dillon Books, 2016) and *Each Crumbling House* (Perugia Press, 2010), winner of the Perugia Press Prize. She is the recipient of Kundiman poetry and fiction fellowships, two Pushcart Prize nominations, and the Robert Watson Literary Prize. Her poems, essays, and reviews appear in *Commonweal Magazine, Blood Orange Review, Lantern Review,* and *The Rappahannock Review.* She is a freelance writer and editor living in St. Louis, Missouri with her husband and daughters.

Printed in the USA
CPSIA information can be obtained
at www.ICGtesting.com
JSHW020757170224
57339JS00005B/188